"THE ESSENCE OF THE YANKEES IS THAT THEY WIN."

—Dave Anderson,
The New York Times

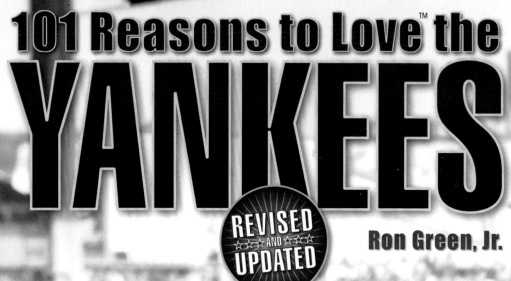

101 Reasons to Love the
YANKEES

REVISED
☆☆ AND ☆☆
UPDATED

Ron Green, Jr.

Stewart, Tabori & Chang
New York

Introduction

It has been more than four decades since I was a seven-year-old growing up in Charlotte, North Carolina, a nice southern town that had no idea it would one day be home to its own major-league sports franchises with their own heroes, heartbreaks, and allegiances. Despite the years, I can still remember sitting in the barber's chair one Saturday afternoon, wishing I had the kind of hair that would allow me to wear a flattop while also thinking how lucky I was that my age matched Mickey Mantle's uniform number.

The Mick was on a flickering black-and-white television that afternoon and happened to hit a home run, and it was hard to find anything wrong with the world. That's an example of how the New York Yankees touched my generation, just as they touched generations before and after. They were not just New York's team, they were — to borrow a hackneyed phrase — America's first team. You didn't have to be from New York to love the Yankees. And you still don't.

I should have been a Minnesota Twins fan, because their Class AA farm team was based in Charlotte and I spent dozens of summer nights at the old Griffith Park, watching Tony Oliva and others pass through on their way to the majors. But I loved the Yankees, largely because of Mantle, but not solely because of him. There were so many reasons — from the Babe to Lou Gehrig to Joe DiMaggio and beyond. And, of course, they won.

They still do. And they don't just win games and world championships. They win summer nights and the dreams of kids and grown-ups everywhere who imagine roaming center field in Yankee Stadium just as Mantle used to do.

Red Ruffing, Joe Gordon,
Bill Dickey, Charlie Keller, and Joe DiMaggio

2 The Highlanders

Before they were the Yankees, they were the Highlanders. For 10 seasons beginning in 1903, the Highlanders played their games in Hilltop Park, which seated approximately 15,000 fans. It all began when American League president Ban Johnson decided to move an existing team from Baltimore to compete with the New York Giants. Frank Farrell and Bill Devery were the original owners, and they paid $18,000 for the franchise, which drew its name from its ballpark's location at the highest point in Manhattan.

3 Jack Chesbro

Chesbro was known as "Happy Jack," the nickname that's on his plaque in the Baseball Hall of Fame. One of the finest pitchers of his era, Chesbro was known for his spitball, which frustrated hitters for years as it dipped and darted near the plate. Chesbro owns the distinction of pitching the first game in Yankees history, on April 22, 1903, but his legacy is one of extended success and one remarkable season. Chesbro won 154 games from 1901 to 1906, and he led each league in winning percentage. It was his 1904 season that will probably remain unmatched. In that season, Chesbro won 41 games, completed 48 of the 51 games he started, and pitched 455 innings.

Jack Chesbro

4 The Polo Grounds

Among the great stadiums in baseball history, few evoke as many wistful memories as the Polo Grounds in upper Manhattan. It was the home of three different teams over a span of more than 50 years, including a relatively brief time as the home of the Yankees. When the Highlanders moved to the Polo Grounds in 1913, they changed their name to the Yankees. They shared the park with the New York Giants, and with its short left- and right-field lines, it soon became a dream park for Babe Ruth. The right-field line was only 258 feet deep, while it was 277 feet to the left-field foul pole. Center field, however, was a canyon, the wall 455 feet from the plate. When the Yankees began outdrawing the Giants in the stadium they shared, Giants owner Charley Stoneham decided he'd had enough. He evicted the Yankees, and after the 1922 season they moved on—to their own place called Yankee Stadium.

5 Babe Ruth

Even now, more than 70 years since he played his last game, Babe Ruth remains the most famous name in baseball history. He dominated a team, baseball, and the Golden Age of sports in America with his oversized personality and style. He was the player everyone wanted to see.

Baseball changed because of Ruth. Though he was an extremely effective pitcher — helping the Boston Red Sox win the 1916 and 1918 World Series — Ruth became a home-run hitter when he came to the Yankees in 1920. From then on, baseball — and the Yankees — were never the same.

The Babe's numbers:
- 714 home runs
- 2,213 runs batted in
- The first player to hit 30, 40, 50, and 60 home runs in a season
- .342 career batting average
- Averaged 50 home runs, 155 RBI, and a .354 batting average from 1926 to 1931

6 The Curse of the Bambino

It was the stuff of legend or witchcraft or skulduggery. It inspired plays and songs and stories. There are those who will tell you it was the single most important event in baseball history, and there are others who will say it was just a coincidence. But if there is any question why the Yankees–Red Sox rivalry may be the most intense in sports, it's not so much what happened in December 1919, but what happened—or didn't happen—after that.

It was on December 26, 1919, that Boston owner Harry Frazee agreed to sell Babe Ruth to the Yankees for $125,000 and a $300,000 loan. At the time, the Red Sox had won five of the 15 World Series played, three of them with Babe Ruth on their team. The Yankees had not won a World Series. Since that day, any member of Red Sox Nation can tell you Boston went 86 long years between World Series titles. The Yankees, meanwhile, have won 26 through 2007.

7 Bobby Veach

He pinch-hit for Babe Ruth on August 9, 1925, the only time the Babe ever had a pinch-hitter.

8 Yankee Stadium

Considered the most famous stadium in the world, Yankee Stadium sits on a 10-acre site in the Bronx that cost $675,000 when it was purchased. Situated between 157th and 161st Streets, Yankee Stadium opened April 18, 1923, having cost $2.5 million to build, and it came to be known as "The House That Ruth Built." The remodeled Yankee Stadium reopened in 1976 (after the Yankees spent two seasons play-ing in Shea Stadium) and remains one of the most recognizable structures in the world. Prizefights, football and soccer games, and papal visits have also taken place in Yankee Stadium.

When the original Yankee Stadium opened, its roofline was encircled by a copper art deco frieze facade that became one of its most recog-nizable features. Through the years, Babe Ruth, Lou Gehrig, Joe DiMaggio, and Mickey Mantle played under the facade. Painted white in 1967 because it had begun to turn green, the facade was removed when the stadium was remodeled in 1976. A replica of the old facade was placed along a 550-foot stretch above the center-field bleachers. Just beyond the facade in center field, the number 4 train rumbles by on its run from Crown Heights in Brooklyn to Van Cortlandt Park in the Bronx. The elevated tracks are as much a part of the place as pin-stripes and the facade.

In 2009, the Yankees will move into a new state-of-the-art facility next door. While much of the existing stadium will be torn down, parts will be retained as a monument to over eight decades of Yankees history.

9 The Bat

Located near the front of Yankee Stadium, the 120-foot-high bat is actually a boiler stack painted to resemble a Louisville Slugger. With Babe Ruth's signature on it, the bat is a favorite spot for fans to have their photo taken.

10 The Short Porch

The right-field bleachers in Yankee Stadium have always tempted left-handed hitters. When the stadium originally opened, the right-field foul pole was only 295 feet from home plate. It has since been lengthened to 314 feet.

"I SWING BIG, WITH EVERYTHING I'VE GOT. I HIT BIG OR I MISS BIG."

—Babe Ruth

Joe DiMaggio batting.

Miller Huggins

11 Miller Huggins

He was known as the "Mighty Mite" because at only 5 feet 6 inches tall, Huggins was a feisty man who wasn't afraid of anyone. A second baseman for 13 seasons in the majors, Huggins came to New York after a stint as player-manager for the St. Louis Cardinals. He managed the Yankees from 1918 through 1929 and led them to six pennants in an eight-year stretch. It was Huggins who managed the Yankees to their first three World Series titles. His enduring place in history is as the manager of the '27 Yankees — the Murderers' Row team — which was built around Babe Ruth and Lou Gehrig.

12 Wally Pipp

Pipp was the Yankees' starting first baseman for 10 seasons until June 2, 1925, when he was replaced in the starting lineup by Lou Gehrig — who played the next 2,130 games there. Pipp's decision to take the day off due to a lingering headache led him to joke that he took "the most expensive aspirin in history." Legend has it that it was Pipp, scouting for Indianapolis to pick up a little extra money, who had discovered Lou Gehrig playing for the Columbia University nine and urged that he be signed to a baseball contract.

"HUGGINS WAS ALMOST LIKE A SCHOOLMASTER IN THE DUGOUT. THERE WAS NO GOOFING OFF."

—Waite Hoyt

13 Lou Gehrig

Known as the "Iron Horse,"
Gehrig played a record
2,130 consecutive games
(surpassed by Cal Ripken, Jr.,
in 1995) while becoming one
of the most famous and admired
players in baseball history. His
achievements were extraordinary:

– 493 home runs
– .340 career batting average
– 13 straight seasons with at least 100
  RBI, including 184 in 1931
– .632 career slugging percentage
– 1,995 career RBI (fifth all-time)
  – Won the American League
    Triple Crown in 1934

No wonder he's still
known as the "Pride
of the Yankees."

"HE JUST WENT OUT AND DID HIS JOB EVERY DAY."

—Bill Dickey

Lou Gehrig crosses home plate as Babe Ruth (no. 3) trots back to the dugout

14 Gehrig's Four-Homer Day

On June 3, 1932, the Yankees' first baseman hit four home runs at Shibe Park in Philadelphia. In his fifth and final at bat, Gehrig's long fly ball to deep center field was caught inches from the fence.

15 Babe Ruth's Called Shot

In the fifth inning of Game 3 of the 1932 World Series, Ruth was facing Cubs right-hander Charlie Root when, with two strikes, he stepped out of the batter's box. Legend has it that Ruth pointed to the center-field bleachers. Others say he pointed to right field. Still others contend he never pointed at anything. Regardless, Ruth delivered a 436-foot home run to right-center field, his 15th and final World Series home run.

"I'M NOT A HEADLINE GUY. I KNOW THAT AS LONG AS I WAS FOLLOWING RUTH TO THE PLATE I COULD HAVE STOOD ON MY HEAD AND NO ONE WOULD HAVE KNOWN THE DIFFERENCE."

—Lou Gehrig

Lou Gehrig and Babe Ruth

16 Lou Gehrig's Farewell

On July 4, 1939, Gehrig—dying from amyotrophic lateral sclerosis, now commonly known as Lou Gehrig's disease—said this to the Yankee Stadium crowd gathered to honor him:

"Fans, for the past two weeks you have been reading about the bad break I got. Yet today I consider myself the luckiest man on the face of the earth. I have been in ballparks for 17 years and have never received anything but kindness and encouragement from you fans."

Less than two years later—exactly 16 years to the day after he replaced Wally Pipp at first base—the 37-year-old Gehrig died.

"THE WAY A TEAM PLAYS AS A WHOLE DETERMINES ITS SUCCESS. YOU MAY HAVE THE GREATEST BUNCH OF INDIVIDUAL STARS IN THE WORLD, BUT IF THEY DON'T PLAY TOGETHER, THE CLUB WON'T BE WORTH A DIME."

—Babe Ruth

1927 Yankees

17 Murderers' Row

The heart of the lineup for the 1927 Yankees included Earle Combs, Tony Lazzeri, Babe Ruth, Lou Gehrig, and Bob Meusel, all of whom batted over .300 for the year. Ruth hammered 60 home runs, Gehrig drove in 175 runs, and Combs recorded 231 base hits — all league highs — as the Yankees captured their second World Series crown.

18 Stars in Stripes

In *Pride of the Yankees*, Gary Cooper played Lou Gehrig — and earned an Academy Award nomination — in the 1942 movie about the Yankees great.

The Yankees were so big in the 1950s they were a smash on Broadway, too. Gwen Verdon made famous the role of Lola in *Damn Yankees*, a musical that ran for more than 1,000 performances.

John Goodman played the bigger-than-life role of Babe Ruth in the 1992 film *The Babe*. It was an improvement on William Bendix's portrayal of the Babe decades earlier.

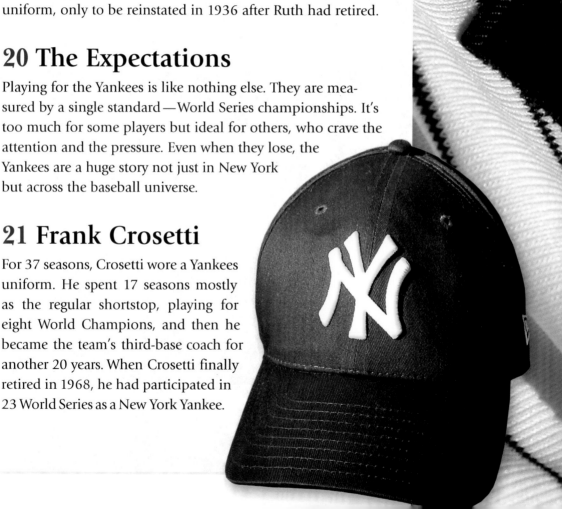

19 The Logo

The interlocking "NY" is instantly recognizable around the world, but, amazingly, Babe Ruth never wore it on his uniform. Before he joined the Yankees, it had been removed from the uniform, only to be reinstated in 1936 after Ruth had retired.

20 The Expectations

Playing for the Yankees is like nothing else. They are measured by a single standard—World Series championships. It's too much for some players but ideal for others, who crave the attention and the pressure. Even when they lose, the Yankees are a huge story not just in New York but across the baseball universe.

21 Frank Crosetti

For 37 seasons, Crosetti wore a Yankees uniform. He spent 17 seasons mostly as the regular shortstop, playing for eight World Champions, and then he became the team's third-base coach for another 20 years. When Crosetti finally retired in 1968, he had participated in 23 World Series as a New York Yankee.

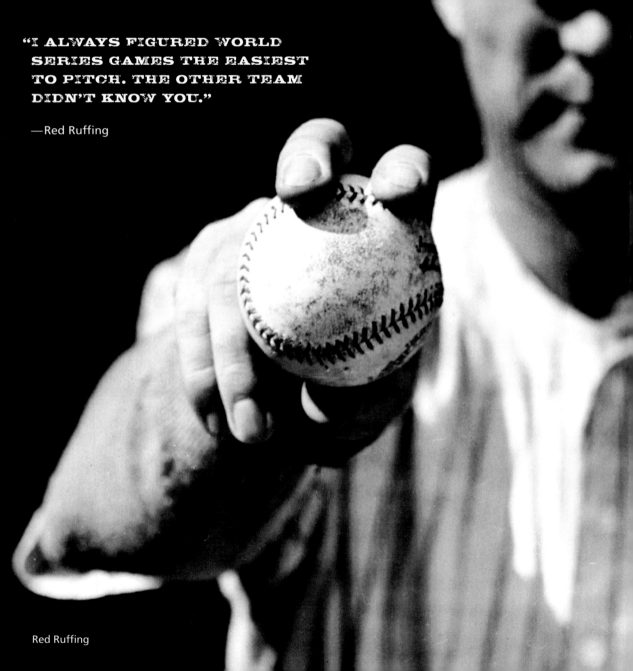

"I ALWAYS FIGURED WORLD SERIES GAMES THE EASIEST TO PITCH. THE OTHER TEAM DIDN'T KNOW YOU."

—Red Ruffing

Red Ruffing

22 Joe McCarthy

Although he never played in the majors, McCarthy earned a place in the Hall of Fame for his work as a manager. McCarthy had a stern, businesslike approach and the bottom line told his story. In 16 seasons with the Yankees (1931–46), McCarthy's teams won 62 percent of their games and seven of eight World Series, including four straight starting in 1936.

23 Red Ruffing

Ruffing was one of the Yankees' all-time great pitchers, going 231–124 during his New York career. He was part of six championship teams and was good enough at the plate that he batted better than .300 eight times.

"I LOVED HIM. ONE OF THE GREATEST MEN I EVER KNEW."

—Tommy Henrich on Joe McCarthy

Joe McCarthy

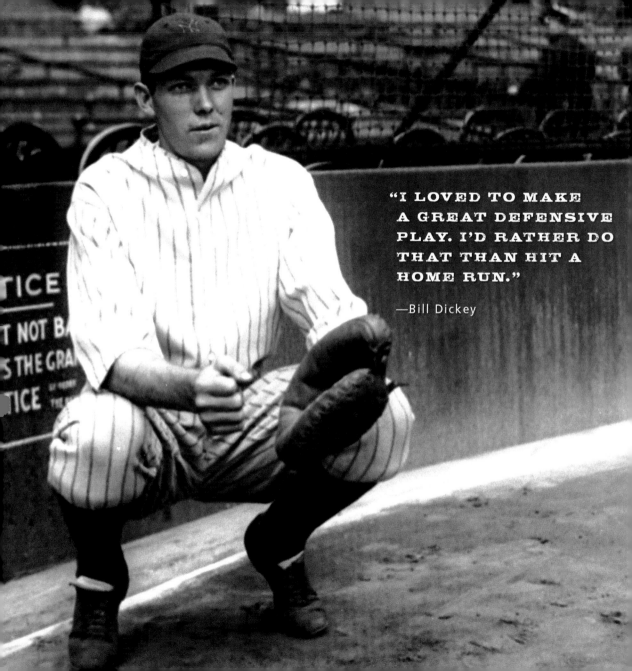

"I LOVED TO MAKE A GREAT DEFENSIVE PLAY. I'D RATHER DO THAT THAN HIT A HOME RUN."

—Bill Dickey

24 Bill Dickey

If the subject is catchers, Dickey's name belongs in the discussion. He was the consummate man behind the plate. With an innate understanding of pitchers, Dickey knew how to manage games, and he was capable of making an impact on them with both his glove and his bat. His .362 batting average in 1936 remains the highest single-season average for a catcher in history.

25 Lefty Gomez

This may say it all about Gomez' career in pin-stripes—his 6–0 record in the World Series is the best in major-league history. Gomez was part of five World Series champions and became the second Hispanic player inducted into the Baseball Hall of Fame.

"THE SECRET OF MY SUCCESS WAS CLEAN LIVING AND A FAST OUTFIELD."

—Lefty Gomez

Lefty Gomez

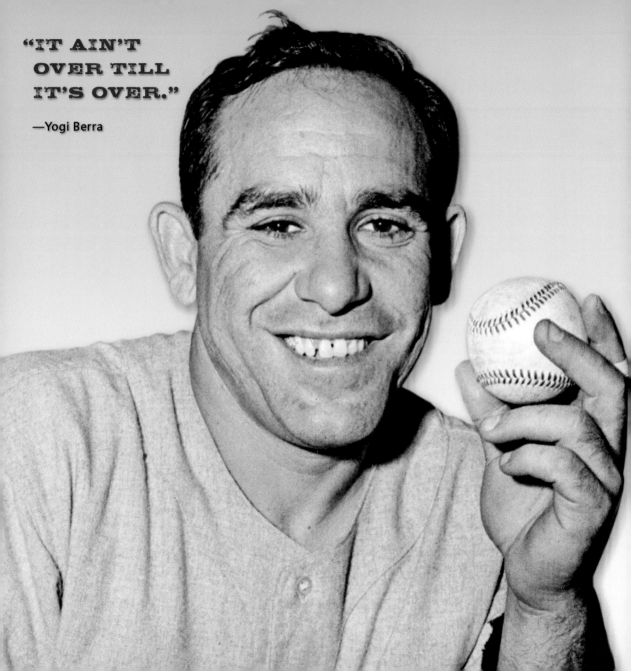

"IT AIN'T OVER TILL IT'S OVER."

—Yogi Berra

26 Monument Park

The history of the great Yankees is honored in the small park located between the bullpens in the Yankee Stadium outfield. It's there that the most famous Yankees are remembered for their contributions with plaques and monuments. In many ways, it's a history of the game. Babe Ruth, Lou Gehrig, Joe DiMaggio, Mickey Mantle—they're each honored there, and so are others whose legacy is part of what has made the Yankees dynasty what it is. Fans arriving early to games can tour the park and be reminded of the legends who helped create baseball's most successful franchise.

27 Yogi Berra

No player in baseball history has won more world championships than Berra, who won 10. Throw in 14 pennants, 15 All-Star Game appearances, a perfect fielding record in 1958, a place in the Baseball Hall of Fame, three MVP awards, and a spot in the hearts of baseball fans everywhere, and it's easy to see why there's never been anyone like Yogi.

28 Yogi-isms

"When you come to a fork in the road, take it."

"You can observe a lot by watching."

"It's déjà vu all over again."

"It gets late early out here."

29 Joe DiMaggio

DiMaggio was a classic in every way. In center field, he could run like the wind to make plays. At the plate, he was among the finest hitters of his or any generation. As a man, he was the consummate gentleman. He even married Marilyn Monroe.

DiMaggio had an amazing grace about him, and, as a personality, he transcended the game that made him famous. The only player ever to make the All-Star team in every season he played (13), Giuseppe Paolo DiMaggio became a touchstone of American culture. He was referenced by everyone from Ernest Hemingway, Woody Guthrie, and Raymond Chandler to *Seinfeld* and *The Simpsons* and, perhaps most famously, when Simon and Garfunkel sang, "Where have you gone, Joe DiMaggio, a nation turns its lonely eyes to you."

"THERE WAS AN AURA ABOUT HIM. HE WALKED LIKE NO ONE ELSE WALKED. HE DID THINGS SO EASILY. HE WAS IMMACULATE IN EVERYTHING HE DID."

—Phil Rizzuto

Joe DiMaggio

30 Joe DiMaggio's Hitting Streak

Of all the great Yankees records, none may be greater than Joe DiMaggio's 56-game hitting streak in 1941. From May 15 through July 16, DiMaggio had a base hit in every game he played, hitting .408 in the stretch.

And when it ended on July 17? DiMaggio went hitless one game—because Cleveland Indians third baseman Ken Keltner made two great plays to rob him of hits—then started another streak of 16 consecutive games with a base hit. Just as impressive was the 61-game hitting streak DiMaggio had as a minor leaguer.

31 The DiMaggio Record

Injuries and a stint in the military limited DiMaggio to only 13 seasons with the Yankees. Of all the numbers he accumulated, the one that mattered most to DiMaggio was this one: the Yankees won nine World Series in his 13 seasons.

"HE WAS BEYOND QUESTION ONE OF THE GREATEST PLAYERS OF THE CENTURY."

—Mickey Mantle

32 Mickey Owen's Dropped Third Strike

Trailing Brooklyn 4–3 in the fourth game of the 1941 World Series, the Yankees were down to their last strike when Dodgers catcher Mickey Owen dropped the third strike on Tommy Henrich, who reached first base. The Yankees scored four runs and won the game.

33 Casey Stengel

As great a character as the Yankees themselves, Stengel managed the Yankees through their exceptional run, adding his own splash of color to the remarkable journey. Stengel was the Yankees' manager from 1949 through 1960, and the numbers his teams accumulated were astonishing. They won 10 American League pennants and seven World Series, including a record five in a row starting in 1949.

"MOST BALL GAMES ARE LOST, NOT WON."

—Casey Stengel

Casey Stengel

Mel Allen

34 The Voices

Broadcasters Mel Allen, Red Barber, and Phil Rizzuto, singer Robert Merrill, and announcer Bob Sheppard. Across the decades, they have told the Yankees' story, on radio, on television, and at the stadium. Their individual styles and personalities have made them as much a part of the franchise as pinstripes.

35 The Scooter

Phil Rizzuto was a part of seven World Series–winning teams during his playing career with the Yankees. He was a classic shortstop, who played with a gritty determination and whose glove skills made him an indispensable part of the lineup. Also a superb bunter, Rizzuto hit .324 in 1950 and handled a record 238 consecutive chances at shortstop without an error, winning the American League MVP award. A five-time All-Star, Rizzuto retired with 1,217 double plays turned, second most in history at the time, and his .968 career fielding percentage remains a glittering testimony to his talent in the field.

"HOLY COW!"

—Phil Rizzuto

Hopalong Cassady

36 Legends Field

It starts each February in Florida at the same place—Legends Field in Tampa. The spring-training home of the Yankees is a place full of possibilities where the playing field has the same dimensions as Yankee Stadium.

37 Hopalong Cassady

Howard "Hopalong" Cassady is known more for his football career—he won the 1955 Heisman Trophy as a running back at Ohio State—than his baseball career, but he's been a part of the Yankees for decades. For years, Cassady has been a special instructor during spring training, and he's a familiar face to most of the players who came through the former Class AAA affiliate in Columbus, Ohio, where he was the longtime first-base coach.

"WHEN THEY WOULD CALL OUT THE LINE-UPS, YOU'D JUST GET THE USUAL CHEERS FOR PLAYERS, NOTHING BIG. AND THEN THEY WOULD CALL OUT THE COACHES AT THIRD BASE AND FIRST BASE. WHEN THEY GOT TO HIM, THE PLACE WOULD GO CRAZY EVERY TIME. IT HAPPENED EVERY NIGHT."

—Andy Phillips

38 Elston Howard

Before he ever played a game for the Yankees, Elston Howard made history. He was the first African-American Yankee. Howard was a quiet man, but his performance on and off the field spoke volumes. He handled the challenges of integration with dignity. In 1963 he became the first African-American to win the American League's Most Valuable Player award.

39 Whitey Ford

Simply put, he was the greatest pitcher in Yankees history. The left-hander spent 16 seasons with the Yankees, amassing 236 victories and a .690 winning percentage that remains the best for any left-hander with at least 200 wins. He was a master on the mound, helping the Yankees win six World Series in the 1950s and 1960s. During the midst of the M&M Boys' great home-run chase in 1961, Ford quietly put together a 25–4 record.

40 Mickey Mantle

A product of the heartland with a name made for a baseball hero, Mickey Mantle may have been the most beloved Yankee of all time. He was both superhuman and utterly human, a combination that endeared him to people who could see beyond the pinstripes and the number 7 to a man who captured the hearts of a generation.

Mantle's numbers were classic:
- 3 Most Valuable Player awards
- 16-time All-Star
- 10 seasons of hitting .300 or better
- 536 career home runs
- 18 World Series home runs

And Mantle himself was a Yankees classic.

"THE ONLY THING I CAN DO IS PLAY BASEBALL. I HAVE TO PLAY BALL. IT'S THE ONLY THING I KNOW."

—Mickey Mantle

Mickey Mantle

41 Mantle's Tape-Measure Home Run

Playing in Griffith Stadium in Washington, D.C., on April 17, 1953, Mantle connected for one of the most prodigious home runs of his career. He slugged a pitch over the left-field wall in the stadium, beyond the bleachers and across the street into a row of houses. The shot was later measured at 565 feet, helping create the mystique of the tape-measure home run.

42 Mantle's 1956 Season

Just entering the prime of his career, Mantle had a season for the ages when he won the Triple Crown while leading the Yankees to their 17th World Series title. Mantle hit .353, slammed 52 home runs, and drove in 130 runs, the most productive season in his career. No wonder, in his prime, Mantle was considered the most powerful hitter in the game, and the fastest.

"AFTER A HOME RUN, I HAD A HABIT OF RUNNING THE BASES WITH MY HEAD DOWN. I FIGURED THE PITCHER ALREADY FELT BAD ENOUGH WITHOUT ME SHOWING HIM UP ROUNDING THE BASES."

—Mickey Mantle

43 Don Larsen's Perfect Game

On October 8, 1956, Larsen pitched Game 5 of the World Series for the Yankees against the Brooklyn Dodgers and retired all 27 batters he faced in order. It is the only perfect game ever thrown in the World Series.

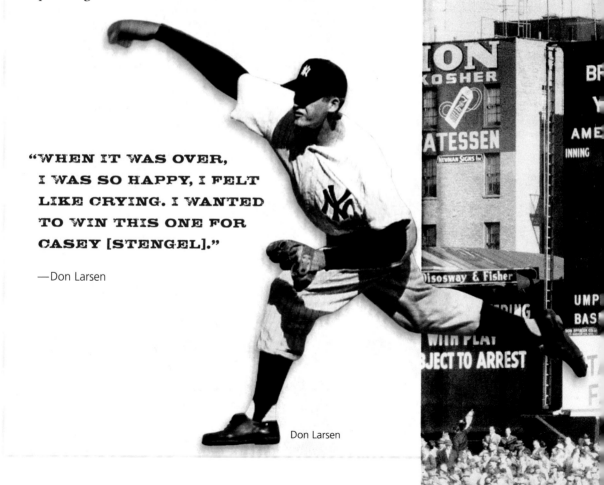

"WHEN IT WAS OVER, I WAS SO HAPPY, I FELT LIKE CRYING. I WANTED TO WIN THIS ONE FOR CASEY [STENGEL]."

—Don Larsen

Don Larsen

44 Roger Maris

There was more to Roger Maris than his 61 home runs in 1961. Playing in the same outfield with Mickey Mantle—one-half of the M&M Boys—Maris was a strong left-handed hitter who was also an excellent right fielder. He never liked the attention and pressure that came with his pursuit of Babe Ruth's record, and it took its toll on Maris. But he endured, as has his place in history.

"I NEVER WANTED ALL THIS HOOPLA. ALL I WANTED IS TO BE A GOOD BALLPLAYER AND HIT 25 OR 30 HOMERS, DRIVE IN A HUNDRED RUNS, HIT .280 AND HELP MY CLUB WIN PENNANTS. I JUST WANTED TO BE ONE OF THE GUYS, AN AVERAGE PLAYER HAVING A GOOD SEASON."

—Roger Maris

45 The Great Home-Run Chase

In 1961, Roger Maris and Mickey Mantle—teammates and good friends—chased Babe Ruth's single-season home-run record. Back and forth they went until September, when health problems forced Mantle to settle for 54 home runs. Maris kept going, and on October 1, 1961, he hit a fourth-inning pitch from Boston pitcher Tracy Stallard into the right-field bleachers in Yankee Stadium—the sixth row of section 33, to be precise—and Babe Ruth's single-season home-run record was broken, by another New York Yankee. And the M&M Boys had a place in history, combining for 115 home runs.

"I DON'T WANT TO BE BABE RUTH. HE WAS A GREAT BALLPLAYER. I'M NOT TRYING TO REPLACE HIM. THE RECORD IS THERE AND DAMN RIGHT I WANT TO BREAK IT, BUT THAT ISN'T REPLACING BABE RUTH."

—Roger Maris

Roger Maris and
Mickey Mantle

46 Mel Stottlemyre

Over the course of two 10-year periods—one as a player, another as a pitching coach—Stottlemyre became part of the Yankees' legacy. He arrived at mid-season in 1964 and helped the Yankees to the World Series. An effective sinker-ball pitcher, Stottlemyre spent 10 seasons pitching for the Yankees, winning 20 games three times and totaling 164 career wins in pinstripes. In 1996, Stottlemyre returned as pitching coach on Joe Torre's staff and played a key role in helping the Yankees win four World Series titles. Stottlemyre also had the thrill of seeing his sons, Todd and Mel Jr., pitch in the majors.

47 *Ball Four*

Jim Bouton had left the Yankees by the time he penned *Ball Four*, one of the most famous sports books of all time. But Bouton's days with the Yankees were remembered in the tale of what baseball can be like from the inside.

48 Mike Kekich and Fritz Peterson

During spring training in 1973, the Yankees pitchers announced they had swapped their wives, their families, and their dogs. How's that for a blockbuster trade?

"YOU SPEND A GOOD PIECE OF YOUR LIFE GRIPPING A BASEBALL AND IN THE END IT TURNS OUT THAT IT WAS THE OTHER WAY AROUND ALL THE TIME."

—Jim Bouton

Fritz Peterson,
right front, with
Mike Kekich
and wives

Chris Chambliss

49 The First Designated Hitter

The designation belongs to Ron Blomberg of the Yankees, who earned the distinction by going one for three against the Boston Red Sox on April 6, 1973.

50 Catfish Hunter

On New Year's Eve, 1974, Jim "Catfish" Hunter helped ignite the free-agent era in baseball when he signed a five-year contract worth $3.75 million. The willingness of the Yankees to seek and sign the best free-agent talent on the market would become an integral part of the club's continued success.

51 Chris Chambliss' Home Run

It was the bottom of the ninth, with the score tied 6–6, in the deciding fifth game of the 1976 American League Championship Series between the Yankees and Kansas City Royals. Chambliss clubbed the pitch from Mark Littell just over the right-field wall, and the Yankees won the American League pennant for the 30th time.

"THE SUN DON'T SHINE ON THE SAME DOG'S ASS ALL THE TIME."

—Catfish Hunter on why he never pitched another perfect game after 1968

Billy Martin and
Reggie Jackson

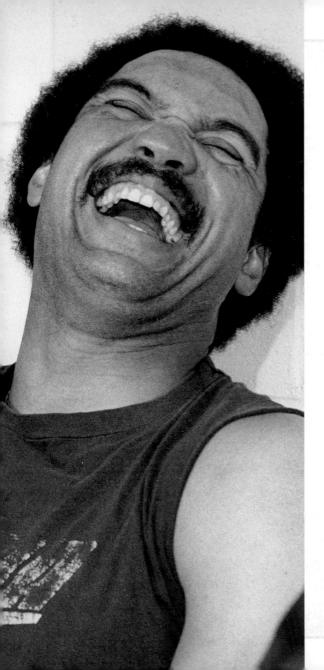

52 The Bronx Zoo

It was the perfect nickname for the franchise in the late 1970s. It seemed that every week another storm would erupt inside the Yankees' locker room or in a New York tabloid. Controversy became the common denominator with the Yankees.

The Yankees were stuffed with over-sized egos and an abundance of talent. The stew created when Billy Martin, Reggie Jackson, Thurman Munson, Sparky Lyle, Mickey Rivers, Lou Piniella, and the others put on the pinstripes read like cheap fiction. They called one another names. They squabbled. They pouted. One Saturday afternoon, Martin and Jackson had to be pulled apart in the Yankee dugout when they went after each other. It was always something. Through it all, the Yankees won consecutive World Series in 1977 and 1978.

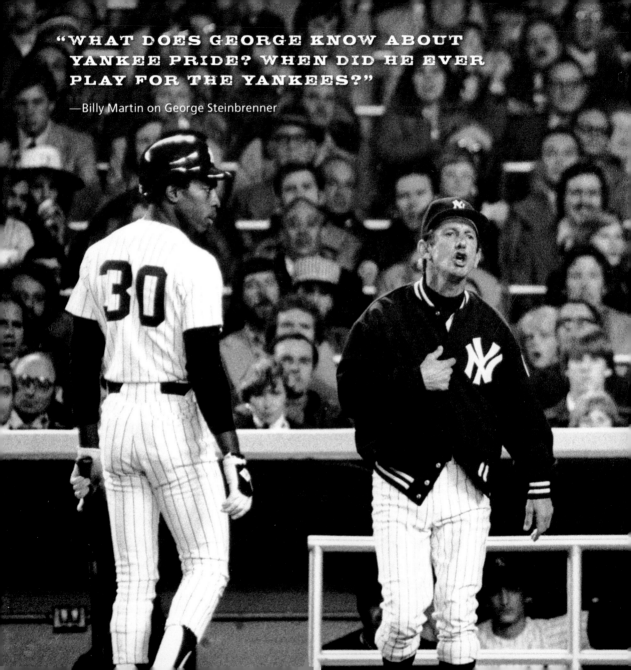

"WHAT DOES GEORGE KNOW ABOUT YANKEE PRIDE? WHEN DID HE EVER PLAY FOR THE YANKEES?"

—Billy Martin on George Steinbrenner

53 Billy Martin

He's hired. He's fired. He's hired. He's fired.

Owner George Steinbrenner hired Martin to manage the Yankees five times, and five times he fired him. It reached the point that the two even made commercials poking fun at how often their relationship switched from hot to cold. Martin, classically tough and combative, managed the Yankees from 1975 to 1978; again in 1979; again in 1983; again in 1985; and again in 1988. The result was two American League championships, the 1977 World Series, and a special place in Yankees history.

His frequent battles with Steinbrenner over-shadowed Martin's long contribution to the Yankees. The team's second baseman in the mid-1950s retired with a career .333 batting average in the World Series, and his feisty style left its mark on the franchise. Despite his temper, Martin became a beloved Yankee and one of Mickey Mantle's closest friends.

54 Reggie Jackson

He called himself "the straw that stirs the drink," and Jackson's five seasons in pinstripes were high drama. Jackson had an ego the size of Manhattan, but he also had an ability to rise to the occasion. He feuded with teammates and with manager Billy Martin, but Jackson found a way to deliver.

Jackson claimed he'd be so big in New York they'd name a candy bar after him — and he was right. When the bar was unveiled in 1978, teammate Catfish Hunter cracked, "Open it and it tells you how good it is." And Jackson showed it. In front of a sellout crowd at Yankee Stadium on a day when everyone had been given a free Reggie Bar, Jackson smacked a three-run homer to beat the Chicago White Sox.

55 "Reg-gie, Reg-gie, Reg-gie!"

Jackson was never better than the night of October 18, 1977, when he homered on the first pitch in three consecutive at bats in Game 6 of the World Series versus the Los Angeles Dodgers, clinching the Yankees' first world championship in 15 years. In fact, Jackson hit four straight home runs, including one in his final at bat in Game 5, forever securing his place as "Mr. October."

"I AM THE BEST IN BASEBALL."

—Reggie Jackson

Thurman Munson

56 Sparky Lyle

He was a symbol of the 1970s with his handlebar mustache and devil-may-care attitude, but when he was on the mound Sparky Lyle knew how to put away baseball games. He became the first relief pitcher to win the Cy Young award when he had 26 saves while helping the Yankees capture the 1977 World Series, ending a 14-year drought between championships.

57 Thurman Munson

Munson was the essence of toughness. With his thick mustache and fierce game face, he was a ferocious competitor. In many ways, Munson was the heart and soul of the Yankees teams that won three straight American League titles (1976–78) and two World Series. He was the Rookie of the Year in 1970 and American League MVP in 1976.

Just the sixth captain in Yankees history, Munson's career was abruptly ended by his death at age 32 when his plane crashed short of the runway at the Akron-Canton, Ohio, Regional Airport on August 2, 1979. Munson's locker remains empty in perpetuity.

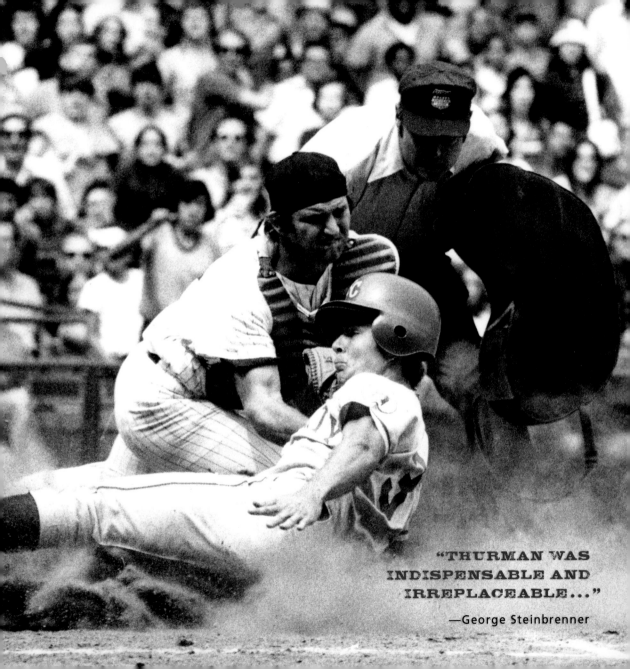

"THURMAN WAS
INDISPENSABLE AND
IRREPLACEABLE..."

—George Steinbrenner

58 Bucky Dent's Home Run

He hit only 27 home runs in his career as a Yankee,
but one is legendary. It came on October 2, 1978, in
the seventh inning of a one-game playoff at Boston's
Fenway Park against Mike Torrez.

The Yankees should have already been finished.
They had trailed the Red Sox by 14 games in the
American League East on July 19, but it was the Red
Sox who had to win their last eight games to force a
one-game playoff for the division title. The Yankees
were down 2–0 when Dent came to the plate in the
top of the seventh with two men on base. The shortstop had batted only .140 in his previous 20 games,
but he drove a 1–1 pitch over Fenway Park's Green
Monster and sent Red Sox Nation into despair.

"BUCKY ****ING DENT."

—Don Zimmer, 1978 Red Sox manager

Ron Guidry

59 Guidry Strikes Out 18 Angels

Ron Guidry set an American League record for left-handed pitchers when he struck out 18 California Angels on June 17, 1978. Guidry, nicknamed "Louisiana Lightning," was virtually unhittable, at one stretch striking out 12 of 13 batters.

60 25–3

In 1978, Ron Guidry had a season as few other pitchers have ever had. He went 25–3 in the regular season with a 1.74 ERA. He allowed just 187 hits in 273 2/3 innings, struck out 248 batters, and walked only 72, while throwing nine shutouts.

61 July 4, 1983

On America's birthday, Dave Righetti pitched the first no-hitter by a left-hander in Yankee Stadium history, shutting down the Boston Red Sox 4–0.

"RON GUIDRY IS NOT VERY BIG, MAYBE 140 POUNDS, BUT HE HAS AN ARM LIKE A LION."

—Jerry Coleman

Dave Righetti

62 Graig Nettles

For 11 seasons, Nettles was the Yankees'
rock at third base. He was an exceptional
fielder, a consistent home-run hitter, and
a fiery personality who earned the rare
honor of being named a Yankees captain.

63 Dave Winfield

He was a star before he joined the Yankees,
and when he signed a 10-year contract with
the club as a free agent, Winfield became
almost bigger than life in a city that loves its
stars. Though he feuded with owner George
Steinbrenner at times, Winfield was an exceptional player who made his mark in the Bronx.
That didn't stop Steinbrenner from occasionally
calling him "Mr. May," a jab in reference to
Reggie Jackson's "Mr. October" moniker, primarily
based on Winfield's poor performance in his only
appearance in a World Series while with the Yankees.

**"WHEN I WAS A LITTLE BOY, I WANTED
TO BE A BASEBALL PLAYER AND JOIN
THE CIRCUS. WITH THE YANKEES, I
HAVE ACCOMPLISHED BOTH."**

—Graig Nettles

Dave Winfield

Goose Gossage

64 Goose Gossage

Big, bold, and full of swagger, Gossage was an intimidating presence on the mound. With a fastball whistling at nearly 100 miles per hour and just a hint of uncertainty about where it might go, Gossage kept opposing hitters on edge. In seven seasons with the Yankees, Gossage had a 2.14 earned run average and 151 saves. He was elected to the National Baseball Hall of Fame in 2008.

65 The Pine Tar Incident

On July 24, 1983, Kansas City's George Brett thought he'd hit a two-out, two-run home run off Goose Gossage to give the Royals a 5–4 lead—until Yankees manager Billy Martin pointed out to umpire Tim McClelland that the extent of pine tar on Brett's bat was in violation of the rules. Brett exploded from the Royals' dugout when the home run was nullified, and he was immediately ejected from the game. The Yankees won 4–3, but American League president Lee McPhail later ordered the game to be resumed from the point following Brett's home run after deciding it should be allowed. The Royals ultimately won, but Brett's reaction rushing from the Yankee Stadium dugout remains a part of baseball history.

"DON'T EVEN INSULT ME BY COMPARING WHAT I USED TO DO TO WHAT THE RELIEVERS DO TODAY."

— Goose Gossage on today's one-inning closers

66 Don Mattingly

He spent 14 years as a player with the Yankees and four more as a coach and owns a special place in the hearts of Yankees fans. "Donnie Baseball" played first base most of his career, winning nine Gold Gloves. Despite being among the most prolific players in franchise history, he never played in a World Series. But with an understated style and professionalism, Mattingly is revered among Yankees faithful. In his prime, before back problems became an issue, Mattingly was an exceptional hitter and won the 1985 AL MVP award. Mattingly's No. 23 was retired, and his plaque in Monument Park speaks to his impact on the franchise: "A humble man of grace and dignity, a captain who led by example, proud of the pinstripe tradition and dedicated to the pursuit of excellence, a Yankee forever."

67 The Nicknames

The Bronx Bombers. Donnie Baseball. Scooter. The Yankee Clipper. The Iron Horse. Murderers' Row. The Sultan of Swat. Mr. October. The Ole Perfessor. The Boss.

"I'M GLAD I DON'T HAVE TO FACE THAT GUY EVERY DAY."

—Dwight Gooden on Don Mattingly

Don Mattingly

"OWNING THE YANKEES IS LIKE OWNING THE MONA LISA."

—George Steinbrenner

George Steinbrenner

68 The Boss

The owner of the New York Yankees since 1973, George Steinbrenner has spent more than three decades as "The Boss." A shipbuilder by trade, Steinbrenner has been aggressive, egotistical, flamboyant, and bullish. He has been suspended and reinstated, cursed and cursed again. But he has always tried to keep the Yankees special, no matter the cost, no matter the situation. Steinbrenner is not just any owner, but the Yankees aren't just any franchise.

69 George Costanza

As the assistant traveling secretary for the Yankees in *Seinfeld*, George managed to mess up everything he touched. He tried to help Danny Tartabull fix his swing, proposed Jon Voight Day at the stadium, and purchased cotton uniforms for the Yankees, which shrank after they were washed. Costanza introduced George Steinbrenner to calzones, but even that backfired.

70 Paul O'Neill

To know what O'Neill meant to the Yankees, all you had to do was look and listen to the stadium crowd at the end of Game 5 in the 2001 World Series. Sensing O'Neill was at the end of his career, the sellout crowd chanted the right fielder's name throughout the ninth inning, bringing tears to the tough guy's eyes. As the Yankees piled up four World Series titles from 1996 through 2000, O'Neill was at the heart of the lineup. He played with an uncommon fire and a toughness that came to define his Yankees teams. O'Neill was a terrific hitter, batting at least .300 for six consecutive seasons in New York, and a solid fielder, but he was more than that. He was a winner.

Joe Torre

71 Joe Torre

When the Yankees hired him before the 1996 season, the first question asked was "Why?" Torre had been a good player and a solid manager, but he hadn't done anything to suggest he would become a legend in pinstripes. With the perfect temperament for managing in the home dugout at Yankee Stadium, Torre made his team a fixture in the postseason, winning three straight World Series, and four of five starting in 1996.

72 A Perfect Dozen

Manager Joe Torre always delivered something more. Torre took over as manager of the Yankees in 1996, and for 12 consecutive seasons he took them into the post-season, winning four World Series and six American League pennants in the process. Few managers in major-league history have been as consistently successful as Torre was in New York, doing it in a time when rosters change constantly.

"HE'S ALWAYS THE SAME. THAT'S THE REASON HE'S BEEN SO SUCCESSFUL....HE'S GOT THE PERFECT MENTALITY, I THINK, FOR A MANAGER."

—Derek Jeter on Joe Torre

73 Derek Jeter

Jeter became the face of a new generation of great Yankees teams and has established himself as one of the most popular and productive players in the history of the franchise. In addition to winning four World Series titles in his first five seasons, piling up three 200-hit seasons in the process, Jeter came to symbolize everything that is great about the Yankees.

Jeter has often been at his best at the biggest moments. His spectacular plays in the field — there was the famous backhand flip to the plate against Oakland in the 2001 ALDS and his full-speed tumble into the stands chasing down a pop-up against Boston — and his gracious style have endeared him to baseball fans around the world.

74 The Captains

There haven't been many: Hal Chase (1912), Roger Peckinpaugh (1914–21), Babe Ruth (1922), Everett Scott (1922–25), Lou Gehrig (1935–41), Thurman Munson (1976–79), Graig Nettles (1982–84), Willie Randolph (1986–88), Ron Guidry (1986–89), Don Mattingly (1991–95), Derek Jeter (2003–present).

"HE'D BEEN SUMMONED
BY THE BASEBALL GODS;
TO CARRY THE TORCH..."

—Peter Richmond on Derek Jeter, *GQ*

Derek Jeter

75 Jeff Maier

The 12-year-old Yankee fan caught Derek Jeter's fly ball at the wall in the first game of the 1996 ALCS, when New York was trailing Baltimore 4–3 in the eighth. Umpires ruled it was a home run though replays showed it was not. The Yankees went on to win 5–4 in 11 innings.

Jeff Maier

76 Jim Leyritz's Home Run

With the Yankees down 2 games to 1 to the Atlanta Braves in the 1996 World Series, and trailing 6–3 in the eighth inning of Game 4, Leyritz smashed a three-run homer that helped New York win the game and, ultimately, another championship.

Jim Leyritz

77 114 Wins

In 1998, the Yankees won 114 regular-season games, capturing the American League East by 22 games. Add in their postseason victories over Texas, Cleveland, and San Diego and the Yankees went 125–50, arguably the greatest season ever for any team.

78 Perfect x 2

On May 17, 1998, Yankees lefty David Wells was perfect against the Minnesota Twins, winning a 4–0 decision while facing the minimum 27 batters in Yankee Stadium. Barely a year later, teammate David Cone duplicated the feat against Montreal. Don Larsen was there and so was Yogi Berra when Cone threw the 16th perfect game in history, beating the Montreal Expos 6–0 on July 18, 1999.

"TO PITCH A PERFECT GAME WEARING PINSTRIPES AT YANKEE STADIUM, IT'S UNBELIEVABLE. GROWING UP A YANKEE FAN, TO COME OUT HERE AND MAKE HISTORY, IT REALLY IS A DREAM COME TRUE."

—David Wells

David Wells

David Cone

79 22–1

Playing in Fenway Park on June 19, 2000, the Yankees handed their bitter rival, the Boston Red Sox, a 22–1 defeat, Boston's worst home loss ever.

Ted Williams, left, and Joe DiMaggio

80 The Red Sox Rivalry

By winning as often as they have, the Yankees have made themselves every team's rival. But there is nothing in baseball—and few like it in any sport—as passionate and enduring as the Yankees and Red Sox rivalry. From the sale of Babe Ruth through Bucky Dent, Aaron Boone, and on to Alex Rodriguez and the stunning 2004 ALCS, it continues in perpetuity, the flame forever burning.

"WITHOUT QUESTION WE'RE TALKING ABOUT THE BEST RELIEVER...IN THE HISTORY OF BASEBALL."

—Brian Cashman on Mariano Rivera

Mariano Rivera

81 Mariano Rivera

From the mid-1990s into the 21st century, Rivera entering the game was a chilling sight to opponents. With wicked control and a cold-blooded approach to his work, Rivera established himself as perhaps the greatest closer in history, doing much of his best work in the postseason.

82 "YMCA"

When the Yankee Stadium grounds crew comes out between innings to smooth the infield during home games, it's a musical number. With the Village People's signature song "YMCA" playing in the stadium, the crew turns an ordinary task into a performance.

83 "New York, New York"

"Start spreading the news..."

84 Bernie Williams

For more than a decade, Bernie Williams played center field for the Yankees with the same smooth style that has made him an accomplished jazz guitarist. A five-time All-Star who played on four world championship teams, Williams' contributions can't be measured purely in numbers. In 1998 he became the only player in history to lead the league in hitting (.339) and win a Gold Glove and the World Series in the same year. The MVP in the 1996 American League Championship Series, Williams is the only player to hit home runs from both sides of the plate in the same postseason game—and he did it twice (the 1995 and 1996 ALDS).

85 Roger Clemens

Already the owner of five Cy Young awards when he joined the Yankees, Roger Clemens wanted what he didn't have—a world championship. He got two of those as a Yankee (1999 and 2000). He also won a sixth Cy Young award, and his one-hit, 15-strikeout shutout of Seattle in the 2000 ALCS remains one of the best postseason pitching performances ever. In 2001, Clemens became the first pitcher in major-league history to post a 20–1 record, doing so with a victory over the Chicago White Sox on September 19. He finished the season at 20–3.

The highlight of Clemens' return to the Yankees in 2007 came on July 2 when he pitched eight innings of two-hit ball to win his 350th game, making Clemens the first pitcher to reach that mark since Hall of Famer Warren Spahn did it in 1963.

86 The Subway Series

For a time, Subway Series were routine in New York City. Before 2000, there had been 13 of them, including seven in a 10-year stretch beginning in 1947. Ten times, the Yankees won the Subway Series, beating either the Dodgers or the Giants in the process. Then, in 2000, the Yankees faced the Mets in a long-awaited renewal of the Subway Series. The city was captivated by the drama, especially when Roger Clemens and Mike Piazza went eye to eye in a classic pitcher-hitter duel. Ultimately, the Yankees won their third straight World Series, beating the Mets 4 games to 1.

Roger Clemens

87 The Derek Jeter Play

It was the kind of play that defines a career. Derek Jeter had already established himself as a Yankees legend, having arrived at shortstop at the start of a great postseason run, and he had shown the knack for making big plays when it mattered the most.

In Game 3 of the 2001 ALDS, trailing the Oakland Athletics 2 games to none, the Yankees were leading 1–0 in the seventh inning when a base hit sent the A's Jeremy Giambi barreling toward home plate with the tying run. In the outfield, Shane Spencer hustled a throw in the general direction of the plate. As Giambi rushed toward the plate with a run that could swing the series, Jeter raced into foul territory to cut off Spencer's throw. With stunning imagination and quickness, Jeter backhanded the ball to catcher Jorge Posada, who laid the tag on Giambi to save the Yankees' win and shift the momentum of the series. The Yankees then won the next two games to advance to the ALCS.

Jorge Posada tags out Jeremy Giambi
as Derek Jeter looks on

88 Aaron Boone's Home Run

It was like Bucky Dent all over again. This time, it was the bottom of the 11th inning in Game 7 of the 2003 ALCS against the Red Sox. All the passion and fire and history between the two franchises seemed to ride on every pitch, every hit, every out. The Red Sox had been five outs away from the World Series, only to surrender three runs in the bottom of the eighth inning when Boston manager Grady Little decided to leave starting pitcher Pedro Martinez in the game, allowing New York to tie the game at 5 and force extra innings. In the bottom of the 11th, Boston sent out knuckleball ace Tim Wakefield to pitch in relief, looking for three more outs to get to the 12th inning. Wakefield threw one pitch, and Boone—who had been acquired earlier in the season in a trade with the Cincinnati Reds—hit it over the left-field wall to give the Yankees their 39th American League pennant.

"IN BOSTON FANS ARE WAILING, AND THEY'RE CURSING AT THE MOON, FOR THERE IS NO JOY IN BEANTOWN THANKS TO AARON BLEEPIN' BOONE."

— John Roche, from www.ultimateyankees.com

Aaron Boone

"I LET THE OTHER GUYS
HANDLE THE TALKING.
I LOVE PLAYING."

—Andy Pettitte

89 Andy Pettitte

Among the most familiar scenes in Yankees baseball has been the image of Andy
Pettitte on the mound in a playoff game, his eyes peering over the top of his glove
as he gets the signal from catcher Jorge Posada. Pettitte, who has earned a reputation
as an exceptional big-game pitcher, spent nine years with the Yankees before leaving
after the 2003 season to play for the Houston Astros. But like his friend Roger
Clemens, who left the same year to play for the Astros, Pettitte returned to New
York in 2007. With 201 career victories at the end of the '07 season, Pettitte needs
only 35 more wins to tie Whitey Ford for the most pitching victories in pinstripes.

90 Jeter, the Mick, and the Prez

When Derek Jeter's 2007 Topps baseball card arrived, it included more than just
the Yankees shortstop. Superimposed in the background was President George W.
Bush, standing in the box seats at Yankee Stadium, missing part of his left arm,
and appearing to be waving to the crowd
while the legendary Mickey Mantle stands
in the dugout holding a bat.

It started as a playful stunt by a card maker
in the company, but when Topps officials
saw it, they decided to make it available.
Collectors pounced on the unconven-
tional card, paying more than $100 in
some cases for it.

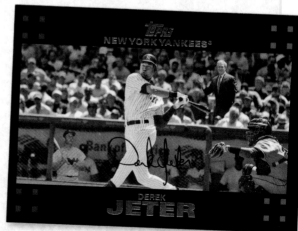

91 Crazy Eights

On July 31, 2007, the Yankees made their game against the Chicago White Sox look like one of those old arcade baseball games you played at the beach, where the silver ball flies out of the park on ramps. The Yankees hit eight home runs in a 16–3 victory over the White Sox, tying a club record set in 1939. Hideki Matsui hit two home runs, while teammates Johnny Damon, Jorge Posada, Bobby Abreu, Melky Cabrera, Robinson Cano, and Shelley Duncan also connected.

92 Godzilla

Before Hideki Matsui joined the Yankees in 2003, he was already a legend in Japanese baseball. He was a three-time MVP of the Japan Central League and led his team, the Yomiuri Giants, to four Japanese World Series. When Matsui signed with the Yankees, it was such a big deal in his homeland that a parade was held in Tokyo to celebrate the event. Matsui, nicknamed "Godzilla," has been a solid contributor to the Yankees' success with his timely hitting, earning him a $52 million contract. He has the distinction of being the first player in franchise history to hit a grand slam in his first game in Yankee Stadium.

"IT'S A PLEASURE TO PLAY OUT THERE WITH HIM. HE'S AS QUIET A SUPERSTAR AS I'VE EVER SEEN ANYWHERE."

—Bernie Williams on Hideki Matsui

Hideki Matsui

"IT WAS AS COMPLETE AN MVP SEASON AS YOU CAN FIND. THE NUMBERS SPEAK FOR THEMSELVES."

—Joe Torre

Alex Rodriguez hitting his 500th home run

93 A-Rod's April

There are good months, great months, and, once in a great while, months like the one Alex Rodriguez had in April 2007. Coming off a disappointing season and having worked himself into exquisite condition, Rodriguez opened the season with a remarkable bang. It started when he homered in the opener versus Tampa Bay, then hit two home runs against Baltimore in the fourth game of the season, the second being a walk-off grand slam, the third of his career. A-Rod had seven home runs in the first 10 games and added another walk-off homer against Cleveland on April 19. When the calendar finally turned to May, A-Rod's numbers included a .355 batting average, 14 home runs (tying Albert Pujols' record), and 34 RBI, one shy of the all-time record.

94 A-Rod's Two-in-One

On the afternoon of September 5, 2007, Alex Rodriguez wasn't sure he'd be able to play that evening against the Seattle Mariners. He underwent an MRI to determine the extent of damage to his ankle after being injured the night before. Upon arriving back at Yankee Stadium with an encouraging report from the examination, A-Rod did some light running and convinced manager Joe Torre he could play that night.

Rodriguez said, "I told [Torre] I could give him some quality at bats."

He did. In a 10–2 victory over Seattle, Rodriguez became the first Yankee since Cliff Johnson 30 years earlier to hit two home runs in the same inning, the seventh. It was another highlight in an MVP season, Rodriguez' third in five years.

95 Jorge Posada

Posada, a product of the Yankees' farm system, became a fixture behind the plate during the team's sustained success under manager Joe Torre. Posada is a five-time All-Star, and his value to the team may never have been greater than in 2007, when he was instrumental in lifting the club back into the playoffs after the team got off to a poor start. Posada hit .395 in September during the Yankees' push to nail down a playoff spot. He became the first catcher ever to hit at least .330 with 40 doubles, 20 home runs, and 85 runs batted in.

96 Manager for a Day

One of Joe Torre's traditions as manager of the Yankees was to allow one of the veteran players to manage the team on the final day of the regular season. Paul O'Neill did it. Roger Clemens did it. Ruben Sierra did it. It was catcher Jorge Posada's turn at the end of the 2007 regular season, and he guided the Yankees to a regular-season-ending 10–4 victory over the Baltimore Orioles. While Torre sat back and watched, Posada—like others before him—learned there's more to managing than he thought.

97 Joe Girardi

When the Yankees chose 43-year-old Joe Girardi to be the 32nd manager in team history, they selected a man with strong ties to the organization, having been a catcher and a bench coach before being hired as Joe Torre's successsor. Known for his toughness and tenacity as a player, Girardi won three World Series champion-ships with the Yankees in 1996, 1998, and 1999, and it's his mission to continue that tradition.

Jorge Posada

Joba Chamberlain

98 Joba Chamberlain

The Yankees discovered a new hero in the latter part of the 2007 season when rookie pitcher Joba Chamberlain arrived on the scene, bringing with him a ferocious fastball and great expectations. Chamberlain became an instant icon among Yankee fans, who learned the story of his life in Nebraska, where he was raised by a single father who was left partially paralyzed by childhood polio. Considered a special talent and perhaps the centerpiece of future Yankee pitching rotations, Chamberlain pitched in relief in 2007 with a strict set of guidelines—known as the Joba Rules—dictating his appearances. The rules, designed to protect Chamberlain's arm, stated that he could only start an inning (rather than be brought in during an inning), he could pitch no more than two innings at a time, and for every inning he pitched, he would have a mandatory day off following his appearance.

99 New Yankee Stadium

In 2009, the Yankees will move into their new stadium next door to where the original Yankee Stadium stands. Leaving the third-oldest park in the major leagues (behind Fenway Park and Wrigley Field) doesn't mean entirely saying good-bye to perhaps the most famous ballpark ever. The new Yankee Stadium will retain the essence of the original while enhancing the experience for spectators and players. The new stadium will have slightly fewer seats than the original but will include 60 luxury boxes and a multitude of restaurants and other activities for spectators. The field will have the same dimensions as the original, the facade will decorate the rooftops, and Monument Park will be relocated to the new stadium. And, next door, much of the original will remain standing. New York City plans to preserve the existing baseball field, dugouts, and some of the stands to be used for Little League and high school games.

100 39 Pennants

1921–23, 1926–28, 1932, 1936–39, 1941–43, 1947,
1949–53, 1955–58, 1960–64, 1976–78, 1981, 1996,
1998–2001, 2003

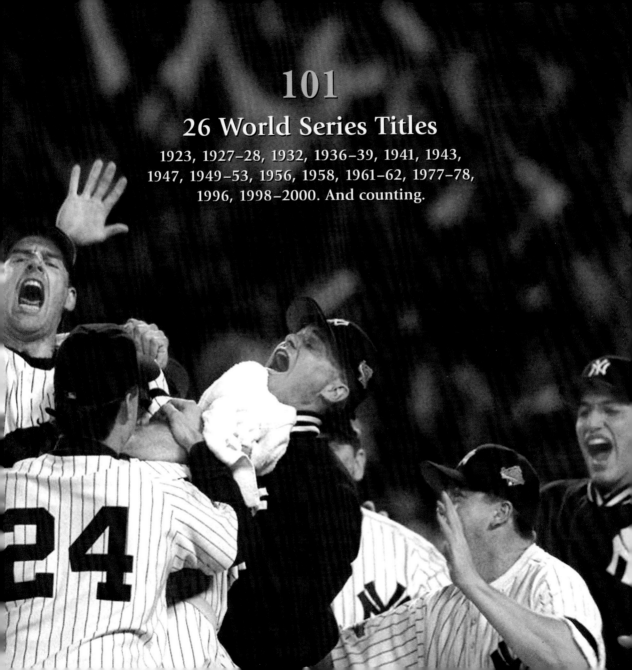

101

26 World Series Titles

1923, 1927–28, 1932, 1936–39, 1941, 1943, 1947, 1949–53, 1956, 1958, 1961–62, 1977–78, 1996, 1998–2000. And counting.

10 Reasons to Hate the Red Sox

Okay, so hate might be a strong word. Or maybe not strong enough. But at the very least, here are 10 reasons to really, really, really dislike the Red Sox. And this is just a start.

1 1919
The Red Sox waited until 1919 to sell Babe Ruth to the Yankees. Just think how many more World Series the Yankees would have won had the Babe joined them earlier.

2 Red Sox Nation
The fans have given themselves a nickname and take a certain amount of pleasure from their long suffering.

3 Monster Seats
They put seats on top of the Green Monster in Fenway Park.

4 Pedro Martinez
Martinez threw Yankees bench coach Don Zimmer to the ground. Okay, so Zimmer shouldn't have come charging like a bull at Pedro, but seriously, he's an old man. At least help him up.

5 A Fashion Don't
Those annoying "Yankees Suck" T-shirts.

6 Ben Affleck

He has become the voice of all things New England and the cleft-chinned face of Red Sox Nation.

7 Bill Buckner

The way Red Sox fans have treated Bill Buckner is disgraceful. Give it a rest. Even if he fielded the ball, the game was going to be tied. The Red Sox still may have blown it.

8 Nomar Garciaparra

The Red Sox traded Nomar Garciaparra. He was classy, gave them the best years of his career, and suddenly they didn't need him anymore. He deserved better treatment.

9 Ted Williams vs. Babe Ruth

The insufferable insistence of Red Sox fans that Ted Williams was the greatest hitter that ever lived. No, he wasn't. Babe Ruth was.

10 2004

The Red Sox completed the greatest comeback in baseball history on Mickey Mantle's birthday when they defeated the Yankees 10–3 in Game 7 of the ALCS after trailing 3 games to none, a feat never before achieved in the major leagues.

Derek Jeter

Acknowledgments

This must begin with a word of thanks to Jennifer Levesque, Leslie Stoker, Galen Smith, and the good people at Stewart, Tabori & Chang, who understand the passion and magic of the New York Yankees. Their commitment to this project is greatly appreciated. And a big thanks to Richard Slovak, our copy editor, who's essential in making sure we get our facts straight and our grammar correct.

Also, thanks go to Mary Tiegreen, whose imagination led to the creation of this book and others like it. In her own way, she has earned her pinstripes.

Thanks to Stan Olson, who knows more about the Yankees than anyone should and who, after all these years, still gets the same charge from them he did as a kid.

A special thank-you to my brother, Dave, who, despite being a Boston Red Sox fan, brought this all together.

To Kevin O'Sullivan and Ted Ciuzio at AP Images, and Bill Burdick and staff at the National Baseball Hall of Fame Library, thank you for all your time and effort.

Also, to my wife, Tamera, and daughter, Molly; my parents, Ron and Beth Green; my sister, Edie, and all the McGlones, as well as the Macchias, you're better than the '27 Yankees.

Of course, no book on the Yankees would be complete without a thank-you to Harry Frazee, the former Boston Red Sox owner, who decided it was a good idea to sell Babe Ruth to the Yankees in 1919.

A Tiegreen Book

Published in 2008 by Stewart, Tabori & Chang
An imprint of Harry N. Abrams, Inc.

Library of Congress Cataloging-in-Publication Data

Green, Ron, 1956-
  101 reasons to love the Yankees /
by Ron Green, Jr. — Rev. ed.
    p. cm.
    ISBN 978-1-58479-715-9
  1. New York Yankees (Baseball team)—Anecdotes.
  2. New York Yankees (Baseball team)—History. I. Title.
    II. Title: One hundred one reasons to love the Yankees.
    III. Title: One hundred and one reasons to love the Yankees.

GV875.N4G72 2008
796.357'64097471—dc22
2008001978

Text copyright © 2008 Ron Green, Jr.
Compilation copyright © 2008 Mary Tiegreen

Editor: Jennifer Levesque
Designer: David Green, Brightgreen Design
Production Manager: Jacquie Poirier

101 Reasons to Love the Yankees is a book in the 101 REASONS TO LOVE™ series.

101 REASONS TO LOVE™ is a trademark of Mary Tiegreen and Hubert Pedroli.

Printed and bound in China
10 9 8 7 6 5 4 3 2 1

HNA ▮▮▮ ▮
harry n. abrams, inc.
a subsidiary of La Martinière Groupe

115 West 18th Street
New York, NY 10011
www.hnabooks.com

Photo Credits

Pages 1, 8, 20, 32, 35, 40, and 71 courtesy of the National Baseball Hall of Fame Library, Cooperstown, New York

Pages 2–3, 4–5, 5 (inset), 6–7, 10, 13, 17, 18–19, 22, 23, 24, 26, 27, 28, 33, 34, 36, 39, 42, 43, 44, 45 (inset), 46, 48, 49, 50, 52, 54 (inset), 55, 56, 59, 61, 62, 64, 66, 69, 73, 74, 75, 76, 77, 78, 81, 82, 84, 87, 88, 89, 90 (inset), 91, 92–93, 94, 97, 99, 101, 102, 105, 106, 109, 110, 112–113, 114–115, 116 (inset), 117 (inset), and 118 courtesy of AP Images

Page 14 courtesy of the Library of Congress Prints and Photographs Division

Pages 30 (cap), 31, 38 (ball), 58 (card), 103 (card), and 120 (card) courtesy of David Green, Brightgreen Design

Page 51 (card) courtesy of Topps Company, Inc.